Grandma
Tell Me
Your Memories

Created by Kathleen Lashier

Copyright © 2012 Linkages

To contact the author:

Linkages Memory Journals • P.O. Box 8282 • Des Moines, IA 50301
888-815-9063
www.mymemoryjournals.com

Printed in the U.S.A.
by G&R Publishing Co.

ISBN-13: 978-1-56383-413-4
ISBN-10: 1-56383-413-8

Distributed by:

CQ Products
507 Industrial Street • Waverly, IA 50677
800-887-4445 • Fax 800-886-7496

*What was your day
and date of birth?*

*Where were you born?
Be specific.*

Do you know any other circumstances of your birth (who was present, who delivered, etc.)?

January 3

If you have a childhood picture for me, put it in this space.

January 4

Name your brothers and sisters and their years of birth.

January 5

*What was your
mother's full name?*

*What were your
mother's date/place and
circumstances of birth?*

*What was your father's
full name?*

_____

_____

_____

_____

_____

_____

_____

_____

_____

_____

January 8

*What was your father's
date/place and
circumstances of birth?*

_____

_____

_____

_____

_____

_____

_____

_____

_____

_____

January 9

Name all the street addresses you can recall and/or all the communities you've lived in and years there.

January 10

January 11

What did your father do for a living?

January 12

Did your mother work outside the home?

Tell a nickname your family gave you and how you got it.

*Tell of any other nicknames
in your family.*

*Tell a fond memory
of your Grandpa.*

*Tell a fond memory
of your Grandma.*

_____

_____

_____

_____

_____

_____

Tell about a favorite Aunt.

_____

_____

_____

_____

Tell about a favorite Uncle.

_____

_____

_____

_____

_____

*Relate an experience
or memory of a cousin.*

January 20

*Did any relatives ever
live with you? If not, then
relate another memory of
cousins, aunts or uncles.*

January 21

In what way did your
mother usually discipline?

How did your
father discipline?

Tell about the naughtiest
thing you ever did.

January 24

If you got caught,
describe the consequences.

January 25

Did you ever see a President
or Vice-President in person?

Which of the Presidents in your
lifetime has been your favorite and why?

January 26

Did you ever have an
imaginary friend?

_____

_____

_____

_____

_____

_____

_____

_____

_____

_____

_____

January 27

What did you and your
brothers or sisters fight
about the most?

_____

_____

_____

_____

_____

_____

_____

_____

_____

_____

_____

January 28

Tell about an experience or
event that drew you together. _____

_____

_____

_____

_____

_____

January 29

Tell about the worst winter storm
that you can remember as a child. _____

_____

_____

_____

_____

January 30

What did you use to go sledding
down a hill in the snow? _____

_____

_____

_____

_____

_____

January 31

What extras did you use for your
snowman's face, buttons, arms, hat, etc?

_____

_____

_____

_____

Tell of someone
you envied, and why.

_____

_____

_____

_____

Do you remember the first movie
you ever saw and who starred in it?

_____

_____

_____

_____

*What have been some of
your very favorite movies?*

*How did you first
smash a finger?*

*Who was the most famous
person you ever met as a child?*

*Tell about someone who had
a big influence on your life.*

Tell about another
influential person in your life.

_____

_____

_____

_____

_____

February 8

Tell about a big lie you told.

_____

_____

_____

_____

_____

February 9

Tell about your first
favorite television shows.

_____

_____

_____

_____

_____

February 10

Who was your first
boyfriend?

Tell about the Valentine
Day festivities at your school.

*Tell about a special
valentine you once gave.*

_____

_____

_____

_____

_____

_____

_____

*Tell about a special valentine
you once received.*

_____

_____

_____

_____

_____

_____

_____

_____

_____

Tell about your first date.

_____

_____

_____

_____

_____

_____

February 15

Tell about your first kiss.

_____

_____

_____

_____

_____

February 16

*What was your favorite
meal as a child?*

_____

_____

_____

_____

_____

February 17

Tell about family reunions
in your childhood.

What do you remember as
your favorite subject in school?

*What do your remember
as your least favorite
school subject?*

*What is the biggest
problem you remember
having in Grade School?*

What is the biggest problem you remember having in Jr. High school?

February 22

What is the biggest problem you remember having in Sr. High school?

February 23

Tell about a great victory or personal success story from your school days.

February 24

Did you and your friends ever have a secret hide-out?

February 25

Tell about a favorite restaurant or public place where you and your friends liked to gather.

February 26

*Tell about the best
pet you ever had.*

*Tell about other
pets you had.*

*Tell about being in a
school play or program.*

*Tell about a school
principal you remember.*

Did you ever pretend to be sick as an
excuse to stay home from school?

_____

_____

_____

_____

_____

_____

March 3

Did you ever get in trouble
for saying a bad word?

_____

_____

_____

_____

_____

March 4

Tell about how you spent your
Saturdays during the school year.

_____

_____

_____

_____

_____

_____

March 5

*Tell about how you
spent your Sundays.*

March 6

*What was the naughtiest or meanest
thing you remember doing in school?*

March 7

*What were the
consequences?*

March 8

Tell of a difficult essay or
term paper assignment.

What radio programs or
stations were your favorites?

Tell of a childhood illness.

Did your parents have a favorite remedy for when you were sick or hurt?

Did kids ever tease
you and why?

Do you remember
your first pizza?

If you went to college, tell which
college you chose and why.

March 15

Tell your major and
how you chose it.

March 16

Did people wear green
on St. Patrick's Day?

March 17

Do you have any other memories
of St. Patrick's Day as a youth? _____

_____

_____

_____

_____

_____

_____

_____

_____

_____

March 18

Describe some household
chores you had as a child. _____

_____

_____

_____

_____

_____

_____

_____

_____

March 19

*Describe some
outside chores.*

_____

_____

_____

_____

_____

_____

_____

_____

March 20

*Which chore did you dislike the most
and how did you try to get out of it?*

_____

_____

_____

_____

Did you have a favorite chore?

_____

_____

March 21

What bones have you
broken and how? _____

_____

_____

_____

_____

March 22

Did you ever
need stitches? _____

_____

_____

_____

_____

March 23

Do you have any other good
stories about being injured? _____

_____

_____

_____

_____

March 24

Tell about an experience
at the doctor's office.

Tell about an experience
at the dentist's office.

What do you remember as your
favorite time of year? Why? _____

_____

_____

_____

_____

_____

_____

_____

_____

_____

March 27

If you ever hitch-hiked, explain. _____

_____

_____

_____

_____

_____

_____

_____

_____

_____

March 28

*Name your best
school friends.*

_____

_____

_____

_____

_____

_____

_____

_____

_____

_____

_____

March 29

*Tell of a nickname given to you by
friends or classmates. How did you
get it? How did you feel about it?*

_____

_____

_____

_____

_____

_____

_____

_____

_____

_____

March 30

What were some crazy names
or nicknames in your school? _____

_____

_____

_____

_____

_____

March 31

Do you have a good
April Fool's Day story? _____

_____

_____

_____

_____

April 1

Tell about a practical joke or
prank you played on someone. _____

_____

_____

_____

_____

April 2

Tell about a practical joke or
prank someone played on you? _____

_____

_____

_____

_____

_____

_____

_____

April 3

Did you ever make a kite?
How? Tell about your _____
kite-flying experiences. _____

_____

_____

_____

_____

_____

_____

April 4

What was your best talent?
What other things were you
really good at doing?

As a child, what did you want
to be when you grew up?

Did you ever bring home or
try to adopt a wild animal?

_____

_____

_____

_____

_____

April 7

Relate a favorite
spring memory.

_____

_____

_____

_____

April 8

Did your Mom or Dad ever find
something you had hidden?

_____

_____

_____

_____

_____

April 9

Make up a limerick about yourself.
There once was a… _____

_____

_____

_____

_____

_____

_____

_____

_____

_____

Now make up a limerick about me.
There once was a… _____

_____

_____

_____

_____

_____

_____

_____

_____

_____

*Share a memory of going to
church as you were growing up.*

April 12

*Share a memory about a
church social activity.*

April 13

Tell about an Easter Egg hunt.

April 14

If your family went to Easter Sunrise services, tell about it.

April 15

Tell about any other
Easter traditions.

_____

_____

_____

_____

_____

_____

_____

_____

_____

_____

_____

April 16

When you played make-believe,
what did you pretend?

_____

_____

_____

_____

_____

_____

_____

_____

_____

_____

_____

April 17

If you could return to your childhood,
what would you do differently?

_____

_____

_____

_____

_____

April 18

Is there anything you would
do differently as a teenager?

_____

_____

_____

_____

April 19

Did you ever write something
that you were really proud of?

_____

_____

_____

_____

_____

April 20

*What is the best book you
ever read as a youth?*

_____
_____
_____
_____
_____
_____
_____
_____
_____

April 21

*Since you've grown, what
has been your favorite book?*

_____
_____
_____
_____
_____
_____
_____
_____

April 22

*Did you have
any superstitions?*

_____

_____

_____

_____

_____

_____

April 23

*Where were your best
hide-and-seek places?*

_____

_____

_____

_____

_____

April 24

*Tell about the first time you were
ever behind the wheel of a car.*

_____

_____

_____

_____

April 25

*Did you ever take anything
that wasn't yours?*

April 26

*What did you do with it?
Did you get caught?*

April 27

*Do you have a story
about a big surprise?*

April 28

*What childhood fear
do you remember?*

April 29

How much do you remember
paying for an ice cream cone?

April 30

Tell about a
May Day tradition.

May 1

What were May Baskets made
of and what did they contain?

May 2

Did you have
a treehouse? _____

_____

_____

_____

_____

_____

_____

May 3

Were you ever
bitten by a dog? _____

_____

_____

_____

_____

_____

_____

May 4

Did your mother ever
make a special gift for you? _____

_____

_____

_____

_____

_____

_____

_____

_____

May 5

Tell a favorite memory
of your mother. _____

_____

_____

_____

_____

_____

_____

_____

_____

May 6

*Tell about some good advice
your mother gave you.*

May 7

*Relate your family Mother's Day
traditions, or tell me more about
what kind of person your mother was.*

May 8

*What did you learn
from your mother?*

May 9

*Name some popular hit
songs from your youth.*

May 10

What was your favorite
singing group or band? _____

_____

_____

_____

_____

_____

May 11

Tell a favorite singer and
a song that he/she sang? _____

_____

_____

_____

_____

May 12

What kind of dances
did you do as a youth? _____

_____

_____

_____

_____

_____

May 13

*Tell about the first
dance you ever went to.*

*Did your high school have
a prom or formal dance.*

*Describe your military
experience or that of
someone in your family.*

*Share a memory involving a war
during your childhood or youth.*

May 16

May 17

What early childhood rhymes
or songs do you remember?

May 18

If you have another photograph of
your childhood to share, place it here.

May 19

What year did you graduate from high school? What do you recall about your feelings, emotions, hopes and dreams at this time of your life?

May 20

May 21

Tell about your graduation exercises or traditions. How many students were in your graduating class?

May 22

Did you have homework
during your school years?

_____

_____

_____

_____

_____

_____

_____

_____

_____

_____

May 23

What was the dumbest stunt pulled
by you and a brother or sister?

_____

_____

_____

_____

_____

_____

_____

_____

_____

May 24

Were there consequences? _____

_____

_____

_____

_____

_____

_____

_____

_____

_____

_____

May 25

*Tell about Memorial Day
traditions during your youth.* _____

_____

_____

_____

_____

_____

_____

_____

_____

May 26

Share a special memory
of Memorial Day.

May 27

Did you play a
musical instrument?

May 28

Tell about the closest friend
you had during your childhood.

May 29

Is there anything you have now that
you have kept from your childhood? _____

_____

_____

_____

_____

_____

_____

_____

_____

May 30

Do you have any good
bathtime stories? _____

_____

_____

_____

_____

_____

_____

_____

_____

May 31

Did you have a favorite nature place you liked to explore?

_____

_____

_____

_____

_____

_____

_____

_____

_____

_____

June 1

Describe a place you liked to go to be alone.

_____

_____

_____

_____

_____

_____

_____

_____

_____

_____

June 2

*Did you ever sleep
under the stars?*

June 3

*Tell about hot dog or
marshmallow roasting.*

June 4

Did you ever go on a
camp out? Tell about it.

_____

_____

_____

_____

_____

_____

_____

_____

_____

_____

June 5

Did you ever go
on a snipe hunt?

_____

_____

_____

_____

_____

_____

_____

_____

_____

June 6

Do you remember a favorite
snack that you liked to make?

June 7

Tell about one of the first
meals you ever prepared?

June 8

What was your first job?
How much did you get paid?

June 9

*Tell about other paying
jobs you had as a youth.*

_____

_____

_____

_____

_____

_____

_____

_____

_____

_____

_____

June 10

*Tell about a strange person
that lived in your town.*

_____

_____

_____

_____

_____

_____

_____

_____

_____

June 11

If you were ever in
a parade, tell about it. _____

_____

_____

_____

_____

_____

_____

June 12

Tell another memory
about a parade. _____

_____

_____

_____

_____

_____

June 13

Share a childhood memory
about a death that affected you. _____

_____

_____

_____

_____

_____

June 14

Relate your happiest
memory as a youth.

June 15

How did you learn to swim?

June 16

Where did you go swimming?

June 17

Tell a favorite memory
of your father. _____

_____

_____

_____

_____

_____

_____

_____

_____

June 18

Tell about some good
advice your father gave you. _____

_____

_____

_____

_____

_____

_____

_____

_____

June 19

Relate your family Father's Day traditions, or tell me more about what kind of person your father was.

_____

_____

_____

_____

_____

_____

_____

_____

_____

_____

_____

_____

June 20

Did your father ever make a special gift for you?

_____

_____

_____

_____

_____

_____

_____

_____

_____

_____

_____

June 21

*What did you learn
from your father?*

*Did you ever go
skinny-dipping?*

Did you ever make mud pies?

Were you ever chased
by an animal?

Did you go barefoot in the summer?
If so, relate an experience about
stepping on something.

June 24

June 25

As a youth, did you do any craft,
sewing, stitching or needlework?

_____

_____

_____

_____

_____

June 26

_____

Tell about a bike you had.

_____

_____

_____

_____

_____

June 27

_____

Tell about your
first very own car.

_____

_____

_____

_____

June 28

*Did you ever have
or make a swing?*

June 29

*Tell about seeing something you
thought was very beautiful.*

June 30

*Describe an outside
game you made up.*

July 1

*Describe an inside
game you made up.*

July 2

*What kind of fireworks did people
have when you were a youth?*

July 3

Tell about Independence Day
traditions of your childhood.

Do you have a special July 4th
that you remember most?

July 4

July 5

*Did you ever go to carnivals
or amusement parks? Where?*

July 6

*What kinds of rides and
games were there? How
much did they cost?*

July 7

*Tell about any State Fair
or County Fair experiences.*

July 8

Tell about going to a circus, a Chautauqua, or a hometown celebration/festival.

July 9

Tell any favorite summertime memory.

July 10

*Did you go fishing, hunting
or trapping in your youth?* _____

_____

_____

_____

_____

_____

_____

_____

July 11

*Tell about your
biggest or best catch.* _____

_____

_____

_____

_____

_____

_____

_____

July 12

*Do you remember having a favorite
candy? How much did it cost?*

July 13

Share a horse-riding story.

July 14

*Share a memory about
going on a picnic.*

July 15

What kinds of party games or
party activities were popular?

_____

_____

_____

_____

_____

_____

_____

_____

July 16

Share a memory involving
a heatwave or drought.

_____

_____

_____

_____

_____

_____

_____

_____

July 17

*What did you
do to stay cool?*

July 18

*What was your favorite
holiday of the year? Why?*

July 19

*Share a birthday
party memory.*

July 20

*Tell about the neatest shoes
you ever owned as a youth.*

July 21

Share a memory
about a power outage.

July 22

Relate a memory involving
a flood or cloudburst.

July 23

Relate a memory of a tornado,
hurricane, or destructive wind.

July 24

What memories do you have of lightning or thunder during your childhood?

_____

_____

_____

_____

_____

_____

_____

_____

_____

July 25

Share a special memory about riding in a boat.

_____

_____

_____

_____

_____

_____

_____

_____

July 26

*Tell about a family
vacation trip.*

July 27

*Share the best vacation
experience you can recall.*

July 28

*Share the most unpleasant
vacation experience you can recall.* _____

_____

_____

_____

_____

_____

_____

_____

July 29

*Do you have any other
memories about a river,* _____
lake, or beach to share? _____

_____

_____

_____

_____

_____

July 30

*Tell a memory about riding
on a ferry, bus, train, or plane.* _____

_____

_____

_____

_____

_____

July 31

Describe a proud moment
from your childhood.

Describe your
childhood home.

Describe your neighborhood.

August 3

Tell about your bedroom.

August 4

Tell a memory about having company
at your house, or of a family party.

_____

_____

_____

_____

_____

_____

_____

_____

_____

_____

_____

_____

August 5

Tell about board games and card
games you played as a youth.

_____

_____

_____

_____

_____

_____

_____

_____

_____

_____

_____

August 6

*Tell about card
games you played.*

*Do you have any
knowledge of how your
first name was chosen?*

*Do you have any knowledge about
the origins of your family name?*

Tell about a time
when you got lost.

Did you ever play in
the sprinkler or hose?

*Share an experience about
poison ivy, poison weed,
bee stings or bug bites.*

August 12

*Did you have any favorite family
songs that you sang together?*

August 13

*Tell of an experience climbing
a mountain or a big hill.* _____

_____

_____

_____

_____

August 14

*Share a memory of staying
overnight with a friend.* _____

_____

_____

_____

_____

_____

August 15

*If you ever ran away
from home, tell about it.* _____

_____

_____

_____

_____

_____

August 16

Do you remember being really
curious about something?

Share your childhood
experiences with roller skates.

August 17

August 18

*Did you ever experience
home sickness?*

*Tell about a favorite,
or least favorite
baby-sitter you had.*

*Share an early experience
with make-up.*

August 21

*Tell about a favorite doll,
teddy bear, or other stuffed toy.*

August 22

*What other toys did
you like to play with?*

August 23

*Did you have to abide
by a curfew as a youth?*

August 24

*Describe any "follow the
leader" games you played.*

August 25

*Phones have changed over the
years. Describe how you used a
phone to call up a childhood friend.*

_____

_____

_____

_____

_____

_____

_____

_____

_____

_____

_____

August 26

*Did you ever have a fire in your home or
accidentally catch something on fire?*

_____

_____

_____

_____

_____

_____

_____

_____

_____

_____

August 27

Tell about going to box socials or pot lucks.

August 28

Tell about an incident when you were very angry with your mom or dad.

August 29

*Tell about an incident when your
mom or dad was very angry with you.*

_____

_____

_____

_____

_____

_____

August 30

*Share a memory
involving an outhouse.*

_____

_____

_____

_____

_____

August 31

*Do you remember any Labor
Day traditions of your youth?*

_____

_____

_____

_____

_____

September 1

*VJ Day...Do you have a memory involving
the end of World War II?
If not, then share a memory of Vietnam.*

*Back-To-School-Days…
What do you remember about that
big yearly "First Day of School"?*

*Tell about your school
year calendar.*

September 4

Tell about a school bully.

September 5

What do you remember
doing at recess?

Tell about the playground
equipment at your grade school.

Did your parents ever make you
wear something stupid to school?

Tell about who you thought was
the smartest kid in school and why.

Tell about the naughtiest
kid in school.

September 9

September 10

*How did you
experience the 9/11 attacks?* _____

_____

_____

_____

_____

_____

_____

_____

_____

_____

_____ *September 11*

_____

_____

_____

_____

_____

_____

_____

_____

_____

_____ *September 12*

Name the schools
that you went to.

_____

_____

_____

_____

_____

_____

September 13

What was your most
embarrassing school moment?

_____

_____

_____

_____

_____

September 14

Where did you usually
buy the clothes you wore?

_____

_____

_____

_____

_____

September 15

*Describe a typical school
day outfit in grade school…* _____

_____

_____

_____

In high school… _____

_____

_____

_____

_____

September 16

*If you were ever in
a fight, tell about it.* _____

_____

_____

_____

_____

_____

_____

_____

September 17

Name the grade school teachers you remember. _____

_____

_____

_____

_____

_____

September 18

Name the Jr. High teachers you remember. _____

_____

_____

_____

_____

September 19

Name the High School teachers you remember. _____

_____

_____

_____

_____

September 20

Tell about a teacher
who meant alot to
you and why.

September 21

If you ever had a hero,
tell who and why.

September 22

Were there any negative role
models who influenced you?

September 23

How did you get to
and from school?

September 24

What were your school colors?

September 25

*What was your
school mascot?* _____

_____

_____

_____

_____

_____

_____

_____

September 26

*Tell any sports you played
in Jr. High or High School.* _____

_____

_____

_____

_____

_____

_____

_____

_____

September 27

*What was your favorite sport
to participate in or watch?*

September 28

*What was the biggest physical
problem you had to deal with?*

September 29

*Do you remember
a school custodian?*

_____

_____

_____

_____

_____

_____

September 30

*What is the worst trick that
you remember a student
playing on a teacher?*

_____

_____

_____

_____

_____

October 1

*What is the meanest thing
you ever saw a teacher do
to a student?*

_____

_____

_____

_____

_____

October 2

Tell about school lunches.
Did you have a lunch box? _____
What did you eat? _____

_____

_____

_____

_____

_____

_____

October 3

Did you ever have
a crush on a teacher? _____

_____

_____

_____

_____

_____

_____

_____

October 4

Do you have any special memories about raking and burning leaves, or mowing the lawn?

October 5

If you ever played in the leaves, tell about it.

October 6

Do you have some
good advice for me?

October 7

October 8

*Share some good advice
that <u>YOU</u> have recieved
in your lifetime.*

October 9

October 10

*Relate a story about a
mouse in the house.*

October 11

What allowance did you get at
different ages during your youth? _____

_____

_____

_____

_____

_____

_____

_____

_____

October 12

Did you have to do
anything to earn it? _____

_____

_____

_____

_____

_____

_____

_____

_____

October 13

Share a memory about
a bat in the house.

October 14

Do you have any advice on how
to be wise with my money?

October 15

Tell about pulling
or losing a baby tooth.

October 16

Did you ever lose something
really important to you?

October 17

Did you ever lose or break something that belonged to someone else?

_____

_____

_____

_____

_____

_____

_____

_____

_____

_____

_____

October 18

Did you ever have a "good friend" who did something mean to you?

_____

_____

_____

_____

_____

_____

_____

_____

_____

_____

October 19

*Share a favorite
fall memory.*

October 20

Did you ever pick apples?

October 21

*What is the farthest you
ever ran or walked?*

October 22

*Did your High School
have cheerleaders?
What did they wear?*

October 23

*Can you recite any
of the school cheers?*

October 24

How did your school observe Homecoming?

October 25

Do you have any special Homecoming experiences to relate?

October 26

Tell about any other High School extra-curricular activities.

_____

_____

_____

_____

_____

_____

_____

_____

_____

_____

October 27

Tell a story about a time when you dressed up in a costume.

_____

_____

_____

_____

_____

_____

_____

_____

_____

_____

October 28

Share a memory about
being very scared.

October 29

What did people
do at Halloween?

October 30

Do you have a special
Halloween memory?

October 31

Did you ever tell ghost stories?

November 1

Do you have a good ghost or haunted house story to relate?

November 2

Tell about how you first met my grandfather?

November 3

What qualities first
attracted you to him?

Tell about your
wedding day.

*What would you like me
to know about my mom?* _____

_____

_____

_____

_____

_____

_____

_____

_____

_____

_____

*What would you like me
to know about my dad?* _____

_____

_____

_____

_____

_____

_____

_____

_____

_____

_____

Tell me about the day I was born. _____

_____

_____

_____

_____

_____

_____

_____

_____

_____

November 8

*Who was president
when you were born?* _____

_____

_____

_____

_____

_____

_____

_____

_____

_____

November 9

When did you cast your first
Presidential vote and for whom?

Veteran's Day…
Name the veterans in your family
and times during which they served.

What was your most prized
possession as a child?

Do you have a story about standing
up against odds for something you
really believed in?

Did you ever feel a hatred for
another person? Explain.

November 12

November 13

November 14

Tell about the best birthday
present you ever received.

Was an injustice
ever done to you?

*Did you ever make a
purchase you later regretted?* _____

_____

_____

_____

_____

_____

_____

_____

_____

November 17

*Tell about a memorable
birthday cake?* _____

_____

_____

_____

_____

_____

_____

_____

_____

November 18

*Have you ever had
a recurring dream?*

November 19

*Many people remember just
what they were doing when they
heard of the assassination of
John F. Kennedy. If you are not
old enough to have that time
etched in your memory, relate
any other childhood story.*

November 20

*Describe a few of the favorite
hair styles of your youth.*

November 21

*Did you have a watch as a
child? What was it like?*

November 22

*Share a memory about
a weather-related school
cancellation.*

November 23

Tell about Thanksgiving traditions of your youth.

November 24

What foods were on your Thanksgiving table?

November 25

Share a favorite
Thanksgiving memory.

November 26

Do you have any ice
skating memories to share?

November 27

*What hobbies or collections
did you have as a youth?* _____

_____

_____

_____

_____

_____

November 28

*Tell about the day
my parent was born.* _____

_____

_____

_____

_____

_____

November 29

*How did you choose the
name for that child?* _____

_____

_____

_____

_____

_____

_____

November 30

*Please list your children's full
names and dates of birth.*

December 1

*On the next pages please share
some stories about my parent.*

December 2

December 3

December 4

December 5

December 6

Pearl Harbor Day…
If you are not old enough to relate
a memory of that day, relate any
other childhood remembrance.

Tell about something you built,
designed, or made as a youth.

Tell about your favorite
stores to browse in as a child. _____

_____

_____

_____

What did you like to look at there? _____

_____

December 9

What did you first buy
using your own money? _____

_____

_____

_____

_____

December 10

Were you ever in a church or school
Christmas or Holiday pageant? _____

_____

_____

_____

_____

December 11

*(If the following Christmas topics do not apply, please share
your special Holiday memories and traditions.)*

When did you put up your Christmas tree?
Where did you get them? _____

_____

_____

_____

December 12

How did you decorate your trees? _____

_____

_____

_____

_____

December 13

Did you hang a Christmas stocking? _____

_____

_____

_____

_____

December 14

*Did your Grandpa or
Grandma ever make gifts
for you? Tell about them.*

December 15

*Did your mom or dad ever
make gifts for you? What?*

December 16

Tell about the best Christmas
present you ever received.

_____

_____

_____

_____

_____

_____

_____

_____

_____

December 17

Tell about something special
you gave to your mom.

_____

_____

_____

_____

_____

_____

_____

_____

_____

December 18

*Tell about something special
you gave to your dad.*

_____

_____

_____

_____

_____

December 19

*Tell about the worst Christmas
present you ever received.*

_____

_____

_____

_____

December 20

*Tell about your experiences
with Santa Claus.*

_____

_____

_____

_____

_____

December 21

*Did you ever go
Christmas caroling?*

_____

_____

_____

_____

_____

_____

December 22

*Did your family observe
the birth of Jesus at
Christmas? In what ways?*

_____

_____

_____

_____

_____

_____

December 23

*Tell about Holiday celebrations
at a relative's house.*

_____

_____

_____

_____

_____

_____

December 24

Do you remember
a "best" Christmas? _____

_____

_____

_____

_____

_____

_____

_____

_____

December 25

Share any other
Christmas memory. _____

_____

_____

_____

_____

_____

_____

_____

December 26

*Is there anything else that
you would like me to know
about your childhood?*

December 27

December 28

Do you remember celebrating any
special wedding anniversaries of
your parents or grandparents?

December 29

What special memories do
you have of New Year's Eve
or New Year's Day?

December 30

If you were to make a New
Year's Resolution this year,
what might it be?

December 31

Memory Journals for Special People

Grandma, Tell Me Your Memories – Heirloom Edition

Grandpa, Tell Me Your Memories – Heirloom Edition

Mom, Share Your Life With Me – Heirloom Edition

Dad, Share Your Life With Me – Heirloom Edition

Grandma, Tell Me Your Memories

Grandpa, Tell Me Your Memories

Mom, Share Your Life With Me

Dad, Share Your Life With Me

To the Best of My Recollection

To My Dear Friend

My Days...My Pictures

My Days...My Writings

My Life...My Thoughts

Sisters

Mom, Tell Me One More Story...Your Story of Raising Me

Dad, Tell Me One More Story...Your Story of Raising Me